St. Patrick's Day

by Janet Riehecky
illustrated by Helen Endres

created by Wing Park Publishers

CHILDRENS PRESS®
CHICAGO

For my son, Patrick, who is the joy of my life.

Library of Congress Cataloging-in-Publication Data

Riehecky, Janet, 1953-
    St. Patrick's Day / by Janet Riehecky ; illustrated by Helen
Endres ; created by Wing Park Publishers.
      p.   cm. — (Circle the year with holidays)
      ISBN 0-516-00696-7
      1. St. Patrick's Day — Juvenile literature.   [1. Saint Patrick's Day.
2. Patrick, Saint, 373?-463?   3. Saints]   I. Endres, Helen, ill.
II. Title.   III. Title: Saint Patrick's Day.   IV. Series.
GT4995.P3R54   1994
394.26'2—dc20   93-47640
                                              CIP
                                              AC

St. Patrick's Day

When John got to school on March 17, he saw something strange. There were green footprints in the hall. John followed them, and they led him right to his first-grade classroom!

Mrs. Ryan, John's teacher, was there. "Most of you know that today is St. Patrick's Day," she said. "I can tell because you're wearing green. And guess what? We have a special visitor today. See if you can find him."

All the boys and girls looked. Dawn looked under the desk. Brandon looked in the wastebasket. John opened the closet. There was a little man dressed in green, sitting next to a golden pot!

"This is Lenny the Leprechaun," said Mrs. Ryan. "He has come to help us celebrate St. Patrick's Day." She opened the lid of Lenny's golden pot. Inside were pieces of paper. Each piece of paper had a number on it.

"Each piece of paper tells us something we can do to celebrate St. Patrick's Day," Mrs. Ryan explained. "John, why don't you draw the first one."

John reached in the pot and pulled the top
piece of paper. It said, *Make a shamrock to
wear.* "What's a shamrock?" he asked.

"A shamrock is a three-leaf clover," said Mrs. Ryan. "It grows in Ireland and is considered good luck. Many people wear shamrocks on St. Patrick's Day." She showed them a picture. Then she gave everyone a piece of green construction paper and a pattern to trace.

The children traced their shamrocks and cut
them out. Then Mrs. Ryan fastened each one
on with a safety pin. Some children also made
shamrocks that they hung on the walls.

"Vince," said Mrs. Ryan, "see what else Lenny wants us to do."

Vince reached in the pot and pulled out the second piece of paper. It said, *Song and dance time.*

All the children gathered in a circle. Mrs.
Ryan taught them to sing, "When Irish Eyes
Are Smiling." Then she showed them an Irish
dance. Everyone wanted to try it.

Then Mrs. Ryan said, "Maria, you choose the next thing to do."

Maria pulled the third piece of paper out of the golden pot. It said, *Find my gold.*

"Legend in Ireland says that if you catch a leprechaun and hold onto him, he has to show you where he hid his pot of gold. Well," said Mrs. Ryan with a smile, "we can play a game a little different from that. You already found Lenny the Leprechaun and his pot, but you haven't found his gold. He has it hidden all over the classroom. Why don't you see if you can find the gold and give it back to Lenny."

Everyone thought this was a great idea. They began searching. "I found a piece," cried Wanda. She held up a candy coin covered with gold foil. It had been in the flower pot by the window.

"I found one too," George shouted. "It was
under the bookcase."

Soon everyone had found at least one coin. The children piled them next to Lenny's golden pot. "We'll save these for refreshment time," said Mrs. Ryan. "I'm sure Lenny will share with all of you.

"Wanda, you found the first piece of gold, so why don't you read the piece of paper numbered four."

Wanda did. It said, *Refreshment time.*

Mrs. Ryan laughed. "OK," she said. Then she took a cloth off a table in the corner and showed everyone the refreshment table. It had been decorated with green crepe paper and pictures of shamrocks. There were green snacks, such as celery, raw broccoli, and olives. There were sugar cookies with green icing. There was also a green cake and a bowl of green punch.

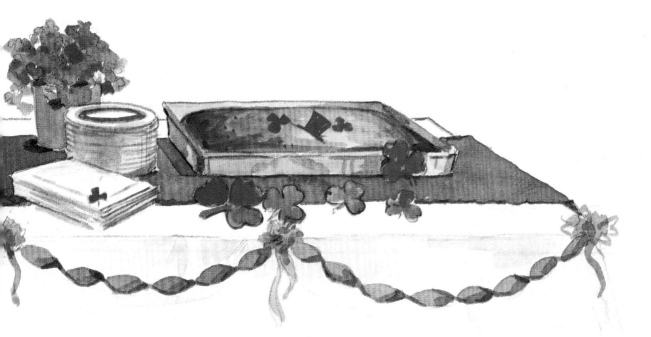

"Mrs. Ryan," Judy asked. "Why is everything green on St. Patrick's Day?"

"Green is a reminder of Ireland," said Mrs. Ryan. "Ireland has beautiful green hills. Many people think the grass there is the most beautiful shade of green in the world.

"On St. Patrick's Day, most people celebrate by wearing green and making everything around them green. In New York City, the Empire State Building puts green lights in its windows at night. In Chicago, they put coloring in the Chicago River and turn it green."

Everyone enjoyed the green snacks. Then
Mrs. Ryan asked Michael to pick the last piece
of paper. It said, *Have a parade.*

"There have been parades on St. Patrick's Day for hundreds of years," said Mrs. Ryan. "The one in New York City is sometimes six hours long. But I think a parade around the school will be long enough for us, don't you?"

The music corner didn't have any bagpipes, but the children grabbed tambourines and cymbals and bells. They marched around the school, singing "When Irish Eyes Are Smiling." It was a great parade.

"I hope you all had fun celebrating St. Patrick's Day," said Mrs. Ryan.

Everyone cheered and clapped, and John
said, "I wish we could have St. Patrick's Day
every day!" Lenny the leprechaun winked!

Activities

A Leprechaun Hat

You can make a tall leprechaun hat to wear at your St. Patrick's Day party. You will need:

—two sheets of green 12″ × 18″ construction paper
—scissors
—glue or tape
—pencil
—measuring tape or ruler

1. Take the first sheet of construction paper and roll it into a tube 12″ tall. Glue the edge so that you have a circle opening at the top and the bottom with a circumference of 17-and-one-half inches.

2. At the top of the tube, cut vertical slits three inches deep, one about every three-quarters of an inch. Bend these toward the center and glue or tape into place, forming the crown of the hat.

3. Take the second piece of construction paper and place the crown of the hat (the first sheet of paper) in the center of it. Trace a circle the size of the bottom opening onto the second sheet. Remove the crown and draw a second circle about three inches larger for the brim of the hat.

4. Cut around the edge of the larger circle. Then poke a hole in the center of the smaller circle and cut slits from the center to the edge of the smaller circle forming triangular tabs. Fold the tabs up and glue or tape them to the inside of the crown. Now you have a tall leprechaun hat!

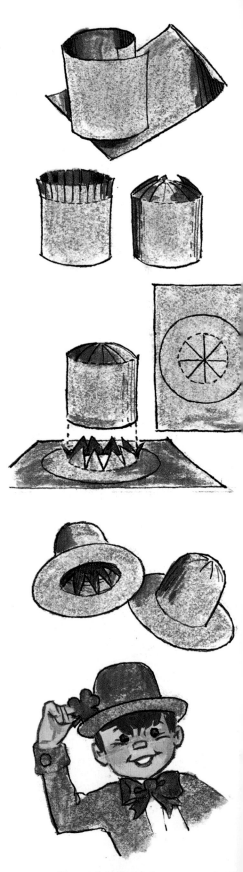

A St. Patrick's Day Placemat

Serve refreshments on these colorful placemats. You will need:

—12" × 18" sheets of dark green and light green construction paper (1 of each color for each placemat).
—scissors
—glue

1. Cut one sheet of paper into strips about one inch wide and twelve inches long.

2. Fold the other sheet of paper in half to make it nine inches by twelve inches. Starting at the folded edge, cut strips about one inch apart, but stop about one inch from the edge, as shown. Open the sheet up.

3. Weave the cut strips over and under the slits as shown. When you are finished with a strip, glue the ends of the strip in place.

4. Decorate your placemat with shamrocks and other St. Patrick's Day pictures.

The Legend of the Shamrock

Tradition tells that when St. Patrick taught the Irish about Christianity, the Irish had trouble understanding the Trinity. St. Patrick looked down at the ground and saw a shamrock, a three-leaf, cloverlike plant. He picked it and explained that the three leaves were like the three persons of the Trinity: God the Father, God the Son, and God the Holy Spirit—three, yet the plant as a whole was one. Since then the Shamrock has been a traditional symbol associated with St. Patrick and with Ireland.

Use this pattern to make little shamrocks to wear; enlarge it to make shamrocks to decorate your classroom.

The Story of St. Patrick

Magonus Succatus Patricius, better known as St. Patrick, was born sixteen hundred years ago in the country that is now England. His family had lots of money and they lived in a big house with lots of servants. But when Patrick was almost sixteen, a terrible thing happened. Invaders came and attacked their country. They kidnapped Patrick and many others and took them to the country that is now Ireland.

Patrick's job was to take care of the pigs, sheep, and cattle. He was lonely and scared. He had to work very hard and he missed his family. Patrick's family were Christians. Patrick had never prayed much when he was a boy, but now he prayed all the time.

For six years Patrick was a slave. Then one night he had a special dream. In the dream he believed God was telling him to escape. So Patrick ran away. It took a long time, but Patrick finally got back to his family. Patrick was happy to be home, but he never forgot the people of Ireland. He became a priest and when the church needed to send someone to Ireland, he returned.

When Patrick went back to Ireland, he taught the people about Christianity. Many, many people decided they wanted to become Christians after they heard what he said. Patrick stayed in Ireland the rest of his life, caring for the people and teaching his faith.

Your class can draw pictures of St. Patrick's life.